W9-ALL-561

Captain John Smith

Discover The Life Of An Explorer

Trish Kline

Rourke Publishing LLC
Vero Beach, Florida 32964

THE PORTRAICTUER OF CAPTAYNE IOHN SMITH ADMIRALL OF NEW ENGLAND.

Æta 37
A° 1616

FROM SOLDIER TO SLAVE

John Smith was born in 1580. He lived in England. When he was 16, John Smith left home to become a soldier. He was a very good soldier. Soon John Smith became a captain in the army. In 1602, he was shot during a battle. The enemy captured John Smith. He was sold as a slave. In 1605, John Smith **escaped** and came back to England.

Before going to the New World, John Smith was a soldier.

TO THE NEW WORLD!

In 1606 Captain John Smith led a group of **settlers**. They sailed to the New World to build a **colony**. In 1607 the ship arrived in the New World. The settlers built a fort and homes. This was the first English colony in America. It was named Jamestown.

Colonists arrived in the New World on ships like these.

SAVED BY A YOUNG GIRL

The winter was very hard. The settlers did not have enough food or fresh water. Many became ill and died.

Native Americans did not like the new settlers. They attacked the settlers over and over. The Native Americans stole the few supplies the colony had.

This picture shows the settlers being attacked.

Captain John Smith went on a hunting trip. He needed to find food for his colony. He was captured by Native Americans. The chief thought Captain Smith should be killed. However, the chief's 11-year-old daughter asked her father to free Captain Smith. The girl who saved Captain Smith's life was Pocahontas.

Pocahontas saved the life of Captain John Smith.

Pocahontas was the daughter of Chief Powhatan.

John Smith explored the coast from Jamestown to New England.

NO WORK, NO FOOD!

When Captain Smith came back to the colony, he found that many of the people had become lazy. They had not hunted. They had little fresh water. They had used nearly all of their supplies. Captain Smith was chosen as leader of the colony. He made a rule that a person must work or else they would not eat. Captain Smith's rules helped the colony to **survive**.

Captain Smith led the colonists at the Jamestown settlement.

AN EXPLOSION

In 1609, a terrible **accident** happened at Jamestown. There was a big **explosion**. Some **gunpowder** blew up. Captain Smith was hurt. His skin was burned very badly. He needed a doctor and **medicine**. But there were no doctors or medicine in the colony. He had to return to England.

Captain Smith set sail for England. He survived but he never returned to the colony in Jamestown.

This statue of Captain John Smith is in Jamestown, Virginia.

LAST ADVENTURE

In 1614 Captain Smith did return to the New World. He landed many miles north of Jamestown. He named the area New England. Today this area is known as Maine and Massachusetts.

Captain Smith wrote many books about New England. People in England read these books. Soon settlers sailed from England to live in New England.

A monument to the first English colony in America stands in Jamestown, Virginia.

LEAVING THE NEW WORLD BEHIND

Captain Smith spent the rest of his life writing. He wrote books about his early trips to Europe and Asia. He also wrote about the settlement of Jamestown.

Captain John Smith was an explorer, soldier, leader, and writer. He died in his homeland of England in 1631. He was 51 years old.

John Smith drew pictures of his adventures in the New World.

IMPORTANT DATES TO REMEMBER

1580	Born in England.
1606	Sailed to the New World to start an English colony.
1607	Captured by Indians. Saved from death by the Indian chief's daughter, Pocahontas.
1609	Hurt in an explosion and returned to England to recover.
1614	Sailed to the New World and named the area New England.
1631	Died in England at the age of 51.

GLOSSARY

accident (AK si dent) — something that happens by mistake

colony (KAHL eh nee) — a place in a country where people live but are ruled by another country

escaped (eh SKAYPT) — broke free from capture, got away

explosion (ik SPLOH zhen) — the act of something blowing up

gunpowder (GUN pow der) — substance used in bullets

medicine (MED eh sin) — substance used to treat illness or injury

settlers (SEH tel erz) — people who made homes in new territories

survive (ser VYV) — to stay alive

INDEX

colony   6, 9, 11, 14, 16, 22

explosion   16

Jamestown   6, 16, 19, 20

Native Americans   9, 11

New England   19, 20, 22

Pochahontas   11, 22

settlers   6, 9, 14, 19

soldier   5

Further Reading

Benjamin, Anne. *Young Pocahontas: Indian Princess*. Econo-Clad Books, 1999.
Sakurai, Gail. *The Jamestown Colony.* Children's Press, 1999.

Websites To Visit

www.encarta.msn.com

About The Author

Trish Kline is a seasoned curriculum writer. She has written a great number of nonfiction books for the school and library market. Her print publishing credits include two dozen books as well as hundreds of newspaper and magazine articles, anthologies, short stories, poetry, and plays. She currently resides in Helena, Montana.